First Facts

American Symbols

The American Flag

by Debbie L. Yanuck

Consultant:
Melodie Andrews, Ph.D.
Associate Professor of Early American History
Minnesota State University, Mankato

Capstone
press

Capstone Press
151 Good Counsel Drive, P.O. Box 669, Mankato, Minnesota 56002
http://www.capstone-press.com

Library of Congress Cataloging-in-Publication Data
Yanuck, Debbie L.
   The American flag / by Debbie L. Yanuck.
   p. cm.—(American symbols)
   Summary: A simple introduction to the American Flag, including its design,
modifications through the years, uses on holidays, and importance as a symbol of the
United States.
   Includes bibliographical references and index.
   ISBN 0-7368-1628-3 (hardcover)
   ISBN 0-7368-4705-7 (paperback)
   1. Flags—United States—History—Juvenile literature. [1. Flags—United States—
History.] I. Title. II. American symbols (Mankato, Minn.)
CR113 .Y36 2003
929.9'2'0973—dc21   2002010708

Editorial Credits
Chris Harbo and Roberta Schmidt, editors; Eric Kudalis, product planning editor;
   Linda Clavel, cover and interior designer; Angi Gahler, illustrator; Alta Schaffer, photo
   researcher

Photo Credits
Capstone Press/Gary Sundermeyer, 5, 18, 19
Corbis/Bettmann, 9
North Wind Picture Archives/N. Carter, 15
PhotoSpin/Joseph Sohm, cover, 7, 21
Stock Montage, Inc., 13
Terwilliger Associates/Mastai Collection, 11, 16, 17
1 2 3 4 5 6 08 07 06 05 04 03

Table of Contents

American Flag Fast Facts

- America's first flag was called the Grand Union flag.

- The Flag Act of 1777 created an American flag with 13 stars and 13 stripes.

- The Flag Act of 1794 created an American flag with 15 stars and 15 stripes.

- In 1949, President Harry Truman declared June 14 National Flag Day.

- Many towns and cities display American flags on Memorial Day, Veterans Day, Flag Day, and other holidays.

- Today, the American flag has 50 stars and 13 stripes. The stars stand for the 50 states. The stripes stand for the original 13 colonies.

American Symbol of Freedom

The American flag is a symbol of freedom. The 13 red and white stripes stand for America's first 13 colonies. These colonies fought for independence from Great Britain. Each of the flag's 50 white stars stands for a state in the United States.

colony
an area that has been settled by people from another country

The Grand Union Flag

The first flags looked different from the flag today. America raised one of its earliest flags during the Revolutionary War (1775–1783). The Grand Union flag had a small British flag in the upper left-hand corner. The rest of the flag had 13 red and white stripes.

Revolutionary War
the war in which the 13 American colonies won their freedom from Great Britain

9

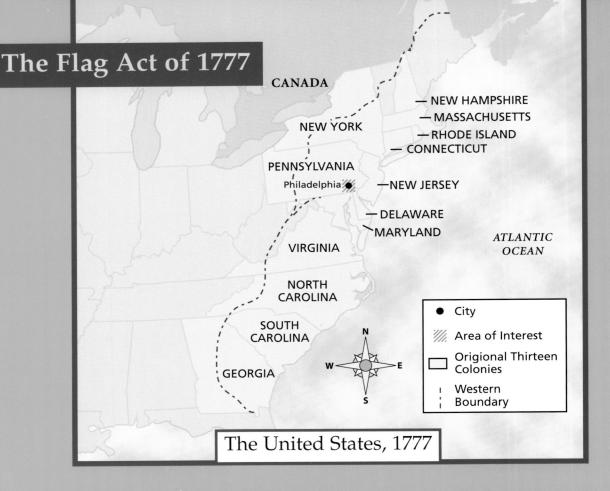

The United States, 1777

On June 14, 1777, the Continental Congress in Philadelphia, Pennsylvania, passed the first Flag Act. This law created a new flag with 13 stars and 13 stripes.

A flag made by a prisoner during the Revolutionary War

The stars and stripes stood for the 13 colonies. The law did not say how the stars should be placed on the flag.

Who Designed the First Flag?

No one is sure who designed the first American flag. Some people say Betsy Ross sewed the first flag. This story is probably not true. Most historians believe Francis Hopkinson designed the first flag. He was a member of Congress from New Jersey.

Hopkinson's design

13

The Flag Act of 1794

By 1792, the United States had grown to 15 states. Some members of Congress wanted two more stars and stripes added to the flag. On January 13, 1794, Congress passed the second Flag Act. This act called for a flag with 15 stripes and 15 stars.

A copy of a flag from 1794

15

The Flag Act of 1818

By 1818, the United States was made up of 20 states. On April 4, 1818, Congress passed the third Flag Act.

A flag from 1818–1819

A flag from 1889

This law gave the American flag 13 stripes again. Congress also could add stars to the flag as new states joined the United States.

People fly American flags many places on special occasions. Many people fly the flag on Memorial Day and Veterans Day.

These holidays honor Americans who died fighting in wars. The flag reminds Americans of the freedom they enjoy today.

Timeline

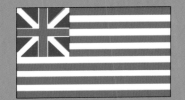

1775—The Revolutionary War begins.

1776—America declares its independence from Great Britain on July 4.

1783—The Revolutionary War ends.

1776—The Grand Union flag is flown over Prospect Hill in Somerville, Massachusetts, on January 1.

1777—The first Flag Act is passed on June 14.

1794—The second Flag Act is passed on January 13.

1949—President Truman signs a bill making June 14 National Flag Day.

1818—The third Flag Act is passed on April 4.

Hands On: Make an American Flag

After 1818, stars were added to the flag each time new states joined the United States. You can make an American flag as it might have looked when your state joined the United States.

What You Need

Craft sticks
Red and white paint
Paint brushes
Scissors

Blue construction paper
Encyclopedia
Craft glue

What You Do

1. Paint seven craft sticks red and six white.
2. Cut a 2-inch by 1.5-inch (5-centimeter by 3.8-centimeter) rectangle from blue construction paper.
3. Look in an encyclopedia to find out when your state joined the United States. How many states were part of the United States when your state joined? If your state was one of the 13 colonies, your flag will have 13 stars.
4. Use a dot of white paint to represent each star on your flag. Put the correct number of dots in rows on the blue square.
5. Glue the 13 craft sticks together side by side. Start with a red stick. Alternate red and white sticks as you glue them.
6. Glue the blue square in the upper left-hand corner of the craft sticks.

Words to Know

Congress (KONG-griss)—the branch of the U.S. government that makes laws

Continental Congress (kon-tuh-NEN-tal KONG-griss)—the group of leaders that made laws for the American colonies

freedom (FREE-duhm)—the right to live the way you want

historian (hi-STOR-ee-uhn)—a person who studies history

honor (ON-ur)—to show respect

independence (in-di-PEN-duhnss)—freedom from the control of other people or things

symbol (SIM-buhl)—an object that stands for something else

veteran (VET-ur-uhn)—someone who has served in the armed forces

Read More

Binns, Tristan Boyer. *The American Flag.* Symbols of Freedom. Chicago: Heinemann Library, 2001.

Gray, Susan Heinrichs. *The American Flag.* Let's See Library. One Nation. Minneapolis: Compass Point Books, 2002.

Internet Sites

Track down many sites about the American flag.

Visit the FACT HOUND at
http://www.facthound.com

IT IS EASY! IT IS FUN!

1) Go to *http://www.facthound.com*
2) Type in: 0736816283
3) Click on "FETCH IT" and FACT HOUND will find several links hand-picked by our editors.

Relax and let our pal FACT HOUND do the research for you!

Index